CANADIAN PACIFIC STEAM
In Color

VOL. 1: MONTREAL & EAST

KEVIN J. HOLLAND

Copyright © 2006
Morning Sun Books, Inc.
All rights reserved. This book may not be reproduced in part or in whole without written permission from the publisher, except in the case of brief quotations or reproduction of the cover for the purposes of review.

To access our full library *In Color* visit us at
www.morningsunbooks.com

ROBERT J. YANOSEY, President

Published by
Morning Sun Books, Inc.
9 Pheasant Lane
Scotch Plains, NJ 07076

Printed in Korea

Library of Congress
Control Number: 2005928876

First Printing
ISBN 1-58248-172-5

Design and production by
Kevin J. Holland
type&DESIGN
Burlington, Ontario

CONTENTS

INTRODUCTION	**3**
CPR STEAM AT SEA	7
INT'L OF MAINE	**12**
NEW BRUNSWICK	**22**
McADAM	24
THE MINTO SUB.	36
THE NORTH END	56
QUEBEC	**58**
QUEBEC CENTRAL	60
SHERBROOKE	82
FARNHAM	88
THE LACHUTE SUB.	93
ST. JEAN/DELSON	106
MONTREAL	**108**

ACKNOWLEDGMENTS

In Canada, as in the United States, the wholesale shift from steam to diesel power during the 1950s galvanized photographers to record the passing of an era. The fires died first in the U.S., and many fans looked north for their final exposure to the steam locomotive in regular mainline service.

Readers of this volume and its companion are indebted to the following photographers, for their wanderlust and skill: Robert F. Collins, George Dimond, Sandy Goodrick, and Preston Johnson. Images not otherwise credited are from the author's collection.

Once again I extend my heartfelt appreciation to publisher Bob Yanosey, for entrusting me with the compilation and production of this project and for allowing two volumes in order to give this remarkable photographic record its due. Through Morning Sun Books, Bob has preserved the increasingly fragile visual record created by an unparalleled fraternity of photographers. Without their combined efforts, it is a record that would otherwise be lost.

DEDICATION

This volume and its companion, along with the previously released *Canadian National Steam in Color, Volumes 1 and 2*, are built largely around the photographic work of the late Robert F. Collins. Along with many of his contemporaries, Bob made numerous trips to Canada in the late 1950s. Not only did he record the changing Canadian railway landscape with sensitivity and skill, but Bob carefully documented the details of what he was recording, knowing, perhaps, that future authors and historians would be grateful for his foresight. This review of Canadian Pacific steam is dedicated to his memory.

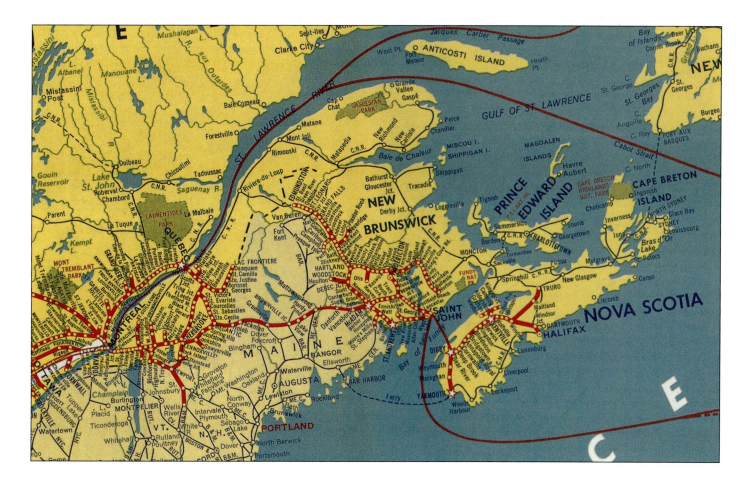

WORLD'S GREATEST TRANSPORTATION SYSTEM

Canadian Pacific at mid-20th century was, literally and figuratively, much more than a railway. As the physical bond that brought British Columbia into the Canadian confederation in the late 19th century, linking the then-isolated West with industrial and financial centers east of the Great Lakes, the Canadian Pacific Railway (CPR) is rightfully accorded credit for its central role in the creation of the Canadian nation as it exists today.

From its earliest years of operation, the CPR's owners and promoters recognized, and exploited, their railway's status as a critical link in the so-called "All-Red Route" of global trade, joining far-flung outposts of the British Empire (shaded red on maps of the period, hence the rosy nickname) via land and sea routes loyal to the Union Jack. The CPR was the means by which generations of European immigrants and settlers were delivered to new lives in eastern Canadian cities and the western Prairies, and also the conduit making it possible for the products of their industrial and agricultural toils to reach markets throughout Canada and the United States. Canadian Pacific management was also quick to identify their railway's potential when it came to that other lucrative passenger: the tourist. Canada's network of spectacular national parks owes much to the CPR, which was built through some of the most breathtaking scenery on the continent.

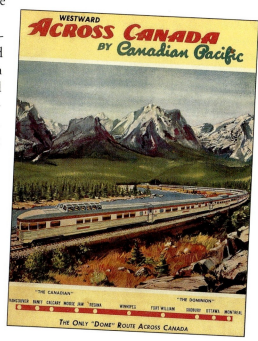

A CANADIAN PACIFIC PRIMER

The Canadian Pacific Railway—today one of the seven surviving major rail carriers in North America—dates to February 15, 1881, when Canada's House of Commons passed legislation enabling the company's creation.

In the years after World War I, Canadian Pacific came to rely heavily on six-coupled steam locomotives. Pacifics and Hudsons handled the vast majority of passenger schedules, and the ubiquitous D10 subclasses of 4-6-0 were regularly assigned to branchline and wayfreight service. Class G1s Pacific No. 2210 was at Woodsville, N.H., on July 9, 1949, while "Royal Hudson" No. 2828 paused at Montreal in March 1958. BOTH, ROBERT F. COLLINS, MORNING SUN BOOKS COLLECTION

The newly formed CPR was handed mileage in British Columbia and Manitoba already contracted by the federal government, and following the appointment of William Cornelius Van Horne as general manager on January 1, 1882, construction across the prairies began in earnest. The year 1883 saw western construction continue well into the Rockies, while acquisition of existing companies gave the CPR the beginnings of its regional route structure in southern Ontario and Quebec.

An 1885 rebellion in Manitoba proved the cash-strapped CPR's strategic worth to the Dominion's security, and federal aid promptly followed to allow completion of a tortuous stretch of track along the north shore of Lake Superior. By the end of that year, the CPR's main line from Montreal to Port Moody (Vancouver) was complete, a symbolic Last Spike was driven at Craigellachie, B.C., on November 7, 1885.

Following several months' work ensuring the line's integrity, North America's first regularly scheduled transcontinental passenger train, the *Pacific Express*, left Montreal on June 28, 1886, arriving in Port Moody on July 4.

Route mileage continued to grow in Ontario and Quebec during 1887 and 1888; on February 1, 1889, the CPR moved its Montreal head offices into the newly opened Windsor Station, which received its first trains three days later.

The railway reached east in 1889 with completion of its "Short Line" route across the state of Maine. The CPR's International of Maine Division, in conjunction with a short stretch of trackage rights over the Maine Central Railroad, linked Montreal with the ice-free Atlantic port of Saint John, New Brunswick, providing the CPR with a winter outlet for freight and passengers when connecting water routes using the St. Lawrence River were ice-bound. Building on its Atlantic bridgehead, the CPR leased the New Brunswick Railway Company on September 1, 1890; this gave Canadian Pacific a network of secondary and branch lines in the western and southern portions of that province.

Route and infrastructure improvements kept pace with growing traffic, particularly in the western mountains, into the first decades of the 20th century; 1909 was a particularly eventful year, with engineering highlights including the opening of the Spiral Tunnels—twin bores built as part of a major grade-reduction effort through British Columbia's Kicking Horse Pass—and a 5,327-foot-long, 314-foot-tall steel viaduct across the Belly River at Lethbridge, Alberta, on the railway's southerly Crows Nest Pass route.

The CPR experienced significant growth through acquisition in 1912, leasing railways in Nova Scotia, Quebec, and British Columbia; although visibly part of the Canadian Pacific "family," the Dominion Atlantic Railway, Quebec Central Railway, and Esquimalt & Nanaimo Railway (the latter on Vancouver Island) were operated as separate subsidiary companies, with much equipment so-lettered.

THE SUM OF THE PARTS

Early in its history, before the turn of the 20th century, managers of the Canadian Pacific Railway sought to create a company catering to virtually every conceivable need of shippers and the traveling public. Whether its patrons sought land, sea, or, after 1942, air travel; highway cartage; a room in an urban hotel; a respite in a scenic mountain or seaside resort; a fine meal; or the means to transfer information or funds, the CPR was ready, willing, and eminently capable of meeting each of these expectations.

Landmark hotels, many built in the copper-roofed "Chateau" style that would become a CPR hallmark, traced their origins to meal stops established when the railway's first trains through the western mountains weren't powerful enough to haul heavy dining cars up the stiff grades. By the end of World War II, the CPR had a major urban hotel in most provincial capitals, and shared operation of the Hotel Vancouver with rival Canadian National—the CNR also maintained a renowned group of hotels and resorts.

Marine operations figured largely in the CPR's integrated network. Its *Empress* liners (see pages 7-9) rivaled

Canadian Pacific's integrated railway, hotel, express, airline, and steamship operations made the company a competitive force at home and around the globe.
AUTHOR'S COLLECTION

the finest competition in Atlantic and Pacific service, while smaller company vessels sailed Canadian coastal and Great Lakes waters; CPR freighters plied the world's oceans as well.

Building on wartime operations ferrying military aircraft from North American factories to Great Britain, Canadian Pacific Airlines emerged under Canada's heavily regulated postwar aviation environment as a largely international carrier, with domestic trunk routes the domain of CNR subsidiary Trans-Canada Air Lines.

Travelers could, literally, circle the earth without leaving the CPR's care.

MOTIVE POWER

For *the* definitive review of Canadian Pacific's steam locomotive history, readers are encouraged to search out a copy of the late Omer Lavallée's comprehensive, 464-page *Canadian Pacific Steam Locomotives*, published by Railfare in 1985. In addition to making sense of the CPR's often convoluted locomotive roster—no small feat, that, given the road's propensity for reclassifications and renumberings prior to World War II—CPR Corporate Archivist Lavallée delves into the personalities behind successive generations of CPR steam power.

Two men, in particular, left considerable legacies following their tenures as the railway's motive power chief. Henry Vaughan, who held the post from 1904 to 1914, oversaw the introduction of the D10 class of 4-6-0; an eventual 502 of the D10 engines were built for Canadian Pacific, many in the railway's own shops, and they performed yeoman's service across the system right until the end of steam. Vaughan also introduced the Pacific to CPR service, in 1906; progressively enhanced over the decades, some of Vaughan's early 4-6-2s also lasted well into the twilight of the steam era, serving alongside examples built as late as 1948.

The man responsible for the final great surge of Canadian Pacific steam locomotive design and production, Henry Bowen, served as motive power chief from 1928 until 1949.

— *continued on page 11*

Canadian Pacific rostered 502 4-6-0s within its various D10 subclasses. At Lawrence, New Brunswick, on March 3, 1960, and with its heavy canvas cab curtain drawn against the cold, D10h No. 1038 led Train No. 91 late in the final winter of CPR steam. ROBERT F. COLLINS, MORNING SUN BOOKS COLLECTION

THE WHITE EMPRESS FLEET

Even after steam locomotives passed from revenue service in 1960, Canadian Pacific continued to employ steam in the movement of passengers and cargo—across the Atlantic, along Canada's Pacific coast, and on the Great Lakes.

Canadian Pacific's role as a pivotal link in the "All Red Route" between Great Britain and its Asian colonies gave the company an ocean-going presence every bit as important as its railway interests. The CPR's marine interests were rooted deep in the company's history, with small vessels employed on the Great Lakes beginning in 1882 to span as-yet incomplete sections of railway. The CPR's first president, George Stephen, had a broader vision, relating to his charge as a "service stretching from Liverpool to Hong Kong."

After several years of employing chartered ships in Pacific service between Canada, Japan, and Hong Kong, the CPR ordered what would become its first three *Empress* liners in October 1889. The *Empress of Japan*, *Empress of India*, and *Empress of China* entered service out of Vancouver in 1891. The *Empress of China* was damaged beyond repair near Tokyo in 1911, but in 1913 two new ships, the *Empress of Asia* and *Empress of Russia*, joined the CPR's Pacific fleet. They were augmented by the *Empress of Canada* and *Empress of Australia* in 1922, and a new *Empress of Japan* in 1930.

Canadian Pacific achieved its directors' longstanding objective of a transatlantic shipping service by acquiring the Elder Dempster Line in 1903. Know as "The Beaver Line," Elder Dempster conveyed 15 ships to the CPR, eight of them passenger liners. The following year, Canadian Pacific built on this start by ordering the first pair of *Empress* liners designed for Atlantic crossings; the *Empress of Britain* and *Empress of Ireland* were delivered in 1906. Further fleet additions were made, through merger and "newbuilding," with older *Empresses* typically renamed or even demoted out of the fleet as newer, larger vessels arrived.

The *Empress of Ireland* met tragedy on May 29, 1914, when it sank after colliding with a coal ship in the St. Lawrence River off Rimouski, Quebec; over 1,000 souls went down with the *Empress*. The late hour and cold water at one of the river's widest points doomed most of those aboard the *Empress*, some of whom undoubtedly chose the ship for what was normally a sheltered 1,000-mile passage from Montreal to the open Atlantic that, in the words of CPR publicists, boasted "39% less ocean" than encountered crossing from New York.

Of the Canadian Pacific *Empresses* in transatlantic service prior to World War II, the best known and most poignantly remembered is the flagship *Empress of Britain*, launched in 1930 as the second CPR ship to bear that name and destined to be the largest passenger vessel to fly the company's distinctive checkered "house" flag.

Into the 1960s, a trio of steam-turbine Canadian Pacific liners linked Montreal with Great Britain via the sheltered "St. Lawrence Route." A 1926 brochure, below, portrayed an earlier *Empress*. AUTHOR'S COLLECTION

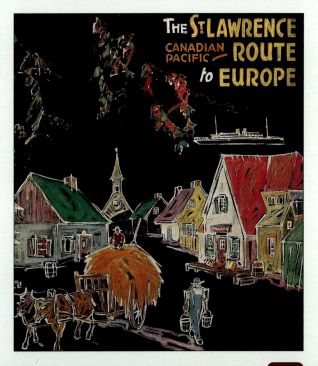

When King George VI and Queen Elizabeth visited Canada in 1939, they arrived at Quebec City aboard the chartered *Empress of Australia* and returned home from Halifax, amid clouds of war, aboard the 42,000-ton *Empress of Britain*. Having developed a well-monied following as an around-the-world cruiser in the early 1930s, the *Empress of Britain* was converted for trooping service with the outbreak of war in September 1939. Barely a year later, on October 26, 1940, a German aircraft dropped a bomb as the unescorted ship neared Ireland. Immobilized and burning, with survivors evacuated, the *Empress* was put under tow; the following day, however, a lurking U-Boat's torpedoes finished her off.

After the war, Canadian Pacific revitalized its transatlantic operation, at first with refurbished veterans like the *Empress of Scotland* (previously the second *Empress of Japan*, and the largest of the CPR's Pacific liners), and *Empress of France* (the CPR's former *Duchess of Bedford*).

Canadian Pacific's "house flag," a red-and-white checkerboard designed by William Van Horne, graced the funnels of the company's ships after World War II, as well as smaller items like stationery, china, and playing cards.

In the early 1950s Canadian Pacific was in the process of modernizing its cross-Canada passenger train operations, having introduced diesel power and ordered 173 stainless-steel cars for its dome-equipped streamliner, *The Canadian*, inaugurated in April 1955. Similar efforts were devoted to a thorough modernization of the CPR's Atlantic liner operation, and orders were placed in 1952 and 1954 for a pair of state-of-the-art ships, destined to become the third *Empress of Britain* and the *Empress of England*. Both ships were built in Great Britain, whose yards had produced most of the world's great ocean liners. The new *Empress of Britain* was a product of the Fairfield Company, while the *Empress of England* was built by Vickers-Armstrong at Walker-on-Tyne.

CPR President N.R. "Buck" Crump lavished attention and funding on his "White Empresses," although he would later reflect on the questionable wisdom of their purchase just as practical jet aircraft were being developed for transatlantic service; even the CPR's airline subsidiary was investigating jets, having ordered the British-built Bristol Britannia four-engine turbo-prop airliner as a competitive stopgap.

The new *Empress of Britain* was launched by Queen Elizabeth II on June 22, 1955, barely two months after *The Canadian* had made its inaugural runs. Less than a year later, the

The largest and most elegant Canadian Pacific liner led a short career marked both by serendipity and tragedy. The *Empress of Britain* entered Atlantic service in 1931 and also made several around-the-world cruises. In the spring of 1939, the ship conveyed King George VI and Queen Elizabeth home to Britain following their landmark tour of Canada and the U.S. Pressed into troop service with the outbreak of war, the *Empress of Britain* was bombed and sunk off Ireland in October 1940.
ALL, AUTHOR'S COLLECTION

wife of British Prime Minister Anthony Eden launched the *Empress of England* on May 9, 1956. These were indeed heady times for Canadian Pacific.

The *Empress of Britain* embarked on her maiden voyage, from home port of Liverpool to Montreal, on April 20, 1956; the *England's* maiden voyage began on April 18, 1957. Essentially sister ships, both were 640 feet long and 85 feet wide.

The final "White Empress" was ordered in January 1958, and christened *Empress of Canada* at launching on May 10, 1960. Her maiden voyage commenced on April 24, 1961. At 650 feet in length, she was the largest of the CPR's postwar trio of new liners, with accommodation for up to 192 first-class passengers and almost 900 in tourist class.

Even as the *Empress of Canada* was under construction, Canadian Pacific's Atlantic operation was feeling relentless pressure from burgeoning air competition and competing shipping lines also experiencing excess capacity on their liners.

In October 1963, the seven-year-old *Empress of Britain* was withdrawn from CPR service and subse-

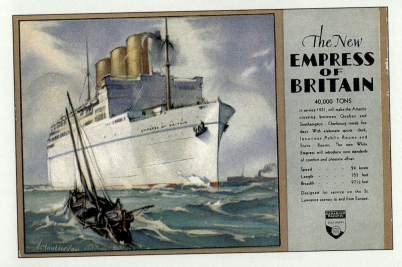

THE WHITE *Empress* FLEET

The newest fleet in the great St. Lawrence-Greenock-Liverpool transatlantic service... Empress of Canada, 27,300 tons... Empress of England and Empress of Britain, each 25,500 tons, gross register... from Montreal every Friday in the St. Lawrence Season! Six luxurious, carefree days to Europe... in the fabulous new world of shipboard life as only Canadian Pacific can offer!

Empress of Britain, royally launched to introduce a new travel era... 640 feet long, 85 feet broad... stabilized! streamlined! stylish! Superbly equipped... for your comfort... for your pleasure... for your safety.

Empress of England, young favourite of transatlantic service and Caribbean Cruises, smart as her sister with First Class and Tourist accommodation to suit most tastes and all purses... weekly, too, between Montreal, Greenock and Liverpool.

Empress of Canada—27,300 gross register tons—650 feet long—86½ feet broad—streamlined—stabilized—for your comfort—between Montreal... Greenock... Liverpool in the St. Lawrence Season—ideal for Caribbean and Mediterranean cruising in winter.

quently sold to the Greek Line, becoming their *Queen Anna Maria*. In late 1975 the ship was again sold, this time to Carnival Cruise Line as the *Carnivale*.

In June 1968, Canadian Pacific introduced new names and color-coded images for its various components; the railway became CP Rail, the airline CP Air, and the oceangoing services were thereafter known as CP Ships.

With new green CP Ships accent colors and the new corporate "Multi-Mark" logo replacing Van Horne's venerable house flag on their funnels, the *Empress of England* and *Empress of Canada* soldiered on for another year or so, providing a leisurely link between Canada and Great Britain and occasional cruises for those who had time to spare.

On April 3, 1970, the *Empress of England* was sold to become Shaw Savill Line's *Ocean Monarch*; scrapping followed in 1975. The *Empress of Canada* closed out the CPR's ocean passenger operations on November 23, 1971. In 1972 she became Carnival's *Mardi Gras*; in painting over the CP Ships funnel markings, Carnival simply rounded the Multi-Mark's contours and changed its colors to create the cruise line's logo that is still in use today.

Canadian Pacific's fleet of steam-turbine *Empresses* numbered only three by 1961. The *Empress of England* and a second *Empress of Britain* were launched as virtual sister ships in 1955 and 1956, and the slightly larger *Empress of Canada* became the last new Canadian Pacific liner in 1960.
BOTH, AUTHOR'S COLLECTION

Like Vaughan before him, Bowen introduced several wheel arrangements—including a revival of the 4-4-4—and improved on his predecessors' best efforts whenever possible.

It was by eschewing an initiative of his immediate predecessor Charles Temple, however, that Bowen molded the final three decades of steam-powered CPR passenger service. Deciding, soon after assuming office, that the two experimental 4-8-4 Northerns (K1a class Nos. 3100 and 3101) developed by Temple were simply too much locomotive for the CPR's needs, Bowen declared the 4-6-4 Hudson his long-distance passenger wheel arrangement of choice. Building on the railway's existing preference for Pacifics in less-demanding mainline roles, Bowen thus cast the six-coupled locomotive to dominate CPR passenger operations, in marked contrast to rival Canadian National's reliance on 4-8-4 and 4-8-2 types. The CNR had been formed soon after World War I from an assortment of financially troubled companies operating long stretches of undermaintained trackage, and eight drivers were an expedient to spread the weight of locomotives large enough to handle the necessary passenger and freight traffic. Through the end of the steam era, Mikados, often double-headed, were the largest power leading CPR freight trains, save for western operations employing a small fleet of T1 class 2-10-4s (another of Bowen's introductions, the oldest dating to 1928).

As North America's railroads embraced streamlining in the early 1930s, Bowen crafted a sleek but restrained countenance that would be shared by his 4-4-4 Jubilees, Hudsons, and later 2-10-4 Selkirks. Due more to its design than its appearance, F2a Jubilee No. 3003 earned headlines on September 18, 1936, when it established a Canadian rail speed record—112.5 m.p.h.—that stood for over 30 years. In a riveted, unstreamlined guise, elements of Bowen's vaguely Anglicized front-end treatment would find their way into selected Mikado and Pacific subclasses as well. That Bowen was still overseeing the creation of new *and* rebuilt steam classes right up until his 1949 retirement spoke volumes to his belief that steam was still the best choice, perhaps not for his industry colleagues, but most certainly for the Canadian Pacific.

Revealingly, however, no sooner had Bowen retired than "young blood" within the CPR—notably future president and chairman N.R. "Buck" Crump—embraced widespread dieselization. That is not to suggest that the railway suddenly rushed ahead; rather, a systematic approach was adopted. The CPR had actually received its first diesel-electric locomotive in December 1937, and followed this hybrid yard unit with orders for more switchers through the war years.

Canadian Pacific steam was officially dead by the end of 1960, despite projections that dieselization would not be complete until the middle of the decade. An economic downturn, the 1959 opening of the St. Lawrence Seaway, and a temporary surplus of diesels on the property were intertwined elements that accelerated steam's demise.

Forty-eight CPR steam locomotives, representing 20 classes, managed to avoid the scrapper's torch, being donated or sold to communities, individuals, and museums in Canada and the United States. While most of these were relegated to the status of dormant park exhibits, 15 have been resurrected at various times for excursion service (although one of these, U3c 0-6-0 No. 6144, was converted to diesel operation).

THE PHOTOGRAPHS

This all-color review of the last decade of Canadian Pacific steam begins not in Canada, but in the United States, with glimpses of the railway's International of Maine (IofM) Division, the busy mainline "shortcut" linking Montreal with Saint John, New Brunswick. Following in the footsteps of the fans and photographers who flocked to the region, the tour enters Canada in southern New Brunswick, where as late as 1960 the CPR continued to operate a handful of 4-4-0s—their origins as old as the company itself—even as diesels bumped heavier and much younger steam power from the region's main lines. Shifting back to the IofM's western end, coverage continues into Quebec, where an assortment of branch and mainline scenes showcase a cross-section of locomotives and trains through the final decade of CPR steam. The tour concludes, for now, in Montreal, Canadian Pacific's longtime headquarters and one of North America's largest and busiest rail centers.

With evidence of a recent snowfall packed in its pilot, G2s Pacific No. 2541 simmered inside the roundhouse at Vallée Jonction, Quebec, on March 1, 1960. The brass builder's plate proudly declares the 4-6-2's birthplace as Canadian Pacific's Angus Shops. ROBERT F. COLLINS, MORNING SUN BOOKS COLLECTION

THE MAINE LINE
East Coast Artery

A mainline link between Montreal and the Atlantic seaport of Saint John, New Brunswick, the CPR's International of Maine Division also provided residents of remote northern Maine with the necessities of everyday life. With "overhead" passengers served during the late steam era by the Montreal–Saint John *Atlantic Limited*, local residents relied on CPR mixed trains M518 and M517—nicknamed the "Scoot"—for their daily-except-Sunday needs. Thanks to the CPR's protracted use of steam, the Brownville Junction, Maine—Mégantic, Quebec mixed trains became the last steam-powered regular-service passenger operation in the United States. On January 1, 1960, class P1d Mikado No. 5107 led the westbound M517 at Jackman, Maine. GEORGE DIMOND

Slicing across the hinterland of northern Maine, the CPR's International of Maine Division was a classic example of what railway promoters of the late 19th century termed an "air line." Taking the most direct, and hence shortest, practicable route between Quebec's Eastern Townships and southern New Brunswick, the IofM gave the CPR a shortcut between its routes in central Canada and the Maritime provinces, avoiding the need of skirting north and then back south around the Pine Tree State's uppermost reaches. Builders of the competing Intercolonial and National Transcontinental railways, meanwhile (both CNR predecessors, and both completed with government funds), were obliged to survey and construct less-direct routes lying wholly within Canada's borders.

Between Mattawamkeag (simply 'Keag to locals) and the border town of Vanceboro, Maine, CPR trains actually traversed the rails of the Maine Central Railroad thanks to a trackage rights agreement that persisted well beyond the end of the steam era. The IofM also connected with the Bangor & Aroostook Railroad at Greenville and Brownville Junction, Maine.

Befitting its status as a mainline artery, the International of Maine hosted a modest assortment of passenger trains during the late steam era. Best-known of the CPR's various Montreal–Saint John schedules over the years was the *Atlantic Limited*, a full-service overnight train inaugurated in 1955 as an upgrading of

ABOVE: As it did elsewhere, the CPR took winter weather in stride on its International of Maine operation. On January 2, 1959, P1e 2-8-2 No. 5137 led eastbound M518 through a squall past westbound counterpart M517 at Brassua, Maine. GEORGE DIMOND

RIGHT: Just over a year later, on March 2, 1960, P1d Mikado No. 5107 had westbound M517 in tow at Jackman. Six hours were allotted for the 117-mile trip between Brownville Junction and Mégantic. ROBERT F. COLLINS, MORNING SUN BOOKS COLLECTION

previously unnamed Trains 41 and 42. A companion Montreal–Saint John schedule, Trains 39 and 40, was discontinued with the debut of the *Atlantic Limited*. With CPR re-equipping its long-distance passenger car assignments using Budd stainless steel rolling stock after 1954, the *Atlantic Limited* earned the distinction as the first and, as long as it was so-equipped, the only dome-equipped train in Maine.

Of the myriad long-distance, multiple-operator passenger trains serving northern New England in the late steam era, only one traveled over a portion of this CPR route. The *Gull* linked Boston's North Station with Halifax, N.S., via an overnight schedule relying on the Boston & Maine, Maine Central, CPR, and Canadian National.

Prior to 1945, the CPR's heavy passenger trains over the IofM were typically led by G2 Pacifics; after the war, members of the road's G3 class became the norm. In perhaps the most marked contrast between the two rivals' post-World War I motive power philosophies, the CPR rostered only two 4-8-4 Northerns, versus more than 200 on the CNR. Virtual orphans among the CPR's Hudson and Pacific passenger-engine fleets, K1a Northerns Nos. 3100 and 3101 were assigned to the Montreal–Saint John passenger schedules in 1954 until the Interstate Commerce Commission, citing concerns of the engines' boilers, barred their use in the U.S.; by this time, diesels were already taking over many IofM passenger and freight assignments.

A lesser light in the CPR's IofM passenger timetable outshone the posh *Atlantic Limited* to become the last regularly scheduled, steam-powered passenger train in the United States. Dubbed the "Scoot," the daily-except-Sunday mixed train between Megantic, Quebec, and Brownville Junction, Maine, was a literal lifeline to year-round and seasonal residents of remote northern Maine before roads gave them alternate access in the 1960s.

Class P1d No. 5107 was wreathed in its own steam at Jackman, Me., on March 2, 1960. The Mikado was built in the CPR's Angus Shops in August 1912. Delivered as No. 5007, it was renumbered in June 1930. Retirement came just over six decades later, in November 1960. ROBERT F. COLLINS, MORNING SUN BOOKS COLLECTION

Canadian Pacific P1d Mikado No. 5107 paused beneath the Stars and Stripes at Jackman, Me., with westbound M517 shortly before noon on March 2, 1960. Near the end of the month, on March 29, this engine led the "Scoot" on its final trip behind steam; that March 29 trip was also the last scheduled passenger train to run behind steam in the United States. A U.S. Customs inspection point, Jackman was also a nocturnal stop for the CPR's Montreal–Saint John *Atlantic Limited*. As far as passengers aboard the "Scoot" were concerned, Jackman was the only positive stop in the 83 miles between Greenville and Mégantic, although 17 flagstops were listed in the CPR's public timetables. Passengers continuing into Canada and west of Mégantic had a convenient connection there with a CPR Budd RDC schedule to Sherbrooke and Montreal. ROBERT F. COLLINS, MORNING SUN BOOKS COLLECTION

ABOVE: Just over 20 miles into its journey on September 4, 1957, CPR westbound M517 passes Bodfish, Me., behind G2s Pacific No. 2584. Built by MLW in 1909 as No. 1234, the 4-6-2 was rebuilt and assigned its final number in 1912. Modernized again and reclassified from G2d to G2s in 1927, No. 2584 was retired in May 1958. GEORGE DIMOND

LEFT: Not reached by road until 1967, Onawa, Me., was a busy stop for the "Scoot." On September 4, 1957, eastbound M518 created a flurry of activity at the remote station. GEORGE DIMOND

TOP: July 1, 1959, saw CPR class G2s Pacific No. 2596 leading eastbound M518 at Jackman. GEORGE DIMOND

MIDDLE: Greenville, Maine, was one of two points—Brownville Junction being the other—where the CPR's International of Maine interchanged with the Bangor & Aroostook through the late steam era. A BAR branch linked Greenville with that road's main line at Derby. On October 7, 1959, Canadian Pacific P1e No. 5137 led M518 past the station; a portion of Moosehead Lake, a popular recreational destination, is visible at right. ROBERT F. COLLINS, MORNING SUN BOOKS COLLECTION

BELOW: Earlier on its journey on the same rainy October day, No. 5137 skirts Long Pond, Me., with the eastbound "Scoot." ROBERT F. COLLINS, MORNING SUN BOOKS COLLECTION

ABOVE: Class G2s 4-6-2 No. 2583 led an orderly M518 at Greenville, Me., on October 6, 1958. Built by MLW in 1909 as CPR G2d No. 1233, the Pacific was officially retired in December 1960. GEORGE DIMOND

LEFT: With CPR dieselization well underway, the products of two builders mingled at Holeb, Me., circa 1958. PRESTON JOHNSON

RIGHT: The victor and soon-to-be vanquished met on the CPR's International of Maine in June 1959, as a through freight behind an FA-1/FB-1 duo stormed past G2s Pacific No. 2596 on the "Scoot." GEORGE DIMOND

Accommodations on the "Scoot" were basic, with reminders of an earlier era to be found in the otherwise Spartan cars' well-tended details. ROBERT F. COLLINS, MORNING SUN BOOKS COLLECTION

NEW BRUNSWICK
Tidewater Tapestry

Canadian Pacific motive power chief from 1928 to 1949, Henry Blane Bowen applied distinctive semi-streamlined styling to several disparate classes of CPR steam, ranging from ponderous 2-10-4 Selkirks and racy Hudsons to diminutive 4-4-4 Jubilees. Of two 4-4-4 classes given the treatment, the 20 members of class F1a, built by the Canadian Locomotive Company in 1937-38, were designed specifically for local and branchline service where light axle loadings were required. Accordingly, members of series 2910-2929 saw service on the CPR's New Brunswick branch lines. On September 5, 1957, the crew of F1a No. 2928 lifted freight cars at Watt, N.B., on their way to St. Andrews. GEORGE DIMOND

Compared to the blanketing route structure of its post-World War I nemesis—the recently amalgamated Canadian National Railways—the CPR's late-steam-era presence in the Maritime provinces amounted to little more than a toehold. Its International of Maine Division mainline route (see pages 12–21) linked Montreal with the ice-free Atlantic port of Saint John, giving the CPR boasting rights as a true ocean-to-ocean transcontinental. A handful of lightly-built branch lines gave the CPR access to rural traffic in southwestern New Brunswick, while a Company steamship connection across the Bay of Fundy between Saint John and Digby, Nova Scotia, linked Canadian Pacific with its Dominion Atlantic subsidiary. (The CPR and DAR lacked a direct land interchange, obliged instead to connect via a circuitous Canadian National route between Saint John, N.B. and Truro, N.S.)

Beyond the Montreal–Saint John main line, light rail and some very light bridge loadings meant correspondingly light power. Canadian Pacific's rural New Brunswick network thus became a time capsule, of sorts, in the late steam era—not only was steam power kept in operation until early 1960, but among the last engines to operate were some as old as the railway itself. Railfans flocked to record the incongruity of archaic but well-maintained 4-4-0s rubbing shoulders with semi-streamlined 4-4-4 Jubilees and other modern power, spanning virtually the entire history of steam locomotive design on the CPR.

RIGHT: Class P2d Mikado No. 5357 was a 1924 product of the Montreal Locomotive Works. On Armistice Day, November 11, 1958, the 2-8-2 awaited its next run at Saint John. ROBERT F. COLLINS, MORNING SUN BOOKS COLLECTION

BELOW: Built in Montreal by the CPR's Angus Shops in 1912, D4g 4-6-0 No. 453 was purchased after its 1960 retirement by renowned photographer O. Winston Link. On November 11, 1957, the engine basked at Saint John. ROBERT F. COLLINS, MORNING SUN BOOKS COLLECTION

Re-entering Canada after passing through Maine, CPR trains reached the bustling division point of McAdam, New Brunswick. From McAdam (known in earlier times as McAdam Junction), the main line continued east to Saint John while branches fed south to St. Andrews and St. Stephen. North of McAdam, a secondary main led north along the international border to Edmunston, N.B., (in part over CNR trackage rights), and also gave access to the provincial capital of Fredericton as well as several short branches.

After 1933 and through the end of the steam era, CPR and CNR passenger trains serving Saint John called at the city's compact Union Station. Canadian Pacific's yard and engine terminal in West Saint John was convenient to the city's (and the CPR's) thriving port facilities; freight transfers to and from the CNR in Saint John were made possible by a bridge spanning the Saint John River at the point where the Bay of Fundy's massive tidal bore altered the channel's flow twice a day to create the famous Reversing Falls.

Steam-powered passenger trains on most of the the New Brunswick secondary lines and branches gave way to gas-electric cars and Budd RDC's before succumbing to rubber-tired alternatives. The *Atlantic Limited*, complete with domes, persisted as a CPR train into the 1970s.

On August 17, 1956, class G2u Pacific No. 2622 prepared to lead the morning's St. Andrews-bound train from McAdam's imposing Canadian Pacific station/hotel. Carrying the markers is a CPR 8 section-1 drawing room-2 compartment sleeper, set out a few hours earlier by the eastbound *Atlantic Limited* from Montreal. Passengers aboard this summer-only *R*-series through sleeper are destined for the Bay of Fundy resort town of St. Andrews, home of the CPR's Algonquin Hotel; the refrigerator cars on the head-end, meanwhile, will be loaded with fish after spotting on the St. Andrews wharf.

BOTH, GEORGE DIMOND

ABOVE: The CPR employed gas-electrics on some of its New Brunswick schedules during the late steam era; No. 9008, an EMC-Ottawa Car Co. model built in 1932, was in McAdam–St. Stephen service on September 5, 1957. GEORGE DIMOND

BELOW: Class G5c Pacific No. 1255, built by the Canadian Locomotive Company (CLC) in November 1946, has arrived at McAdam on August 19, 1953. GEORGE DIMOND

OPPOSITE TOP: Assigned to local duties on August 19, 1953, N2a Consolidation No. 3624 was another CLC product, delivered to the CPR by the Kingston, Ont., builder in August 1911. GEORGE DIMOND

Bound for St. Stephen—a border town opposite Calais, Maine—on August 17, 1956, F1a No. 2928 simmers beside McAdam's station. The CPR designated its two classes of semi-streamlined 4-4-4s as Jubilees, commemorating their 1936 debut during the railway's 50th anniversary year. GEORGE DIMOND

ABOVE: Class N2a Consolidation No. 3632 was switching in the vicinity of McAdam station on August 17, 1956. GEORGE DIMOND

BELOW: At the McAdam engine terminal on the same day, P2b Mikado No. 5319 awaited its next call west. The 2-8-2 was one of 15 classmates built by MLW in 1920–21. GEORGE DIMOND

OPPOSITE: Built in 1912 during the administration of Henry H. Vaughan as CPR motive power chief, G2e Pacific No. 1222 became G2u No. 2622 following a May 1928 rebuilding that included new, larger cylinders. The engine's rounded vestibule cab is original; Elesco feedwater heater and centered headlight were latter-day alterations BOTH, GEORGE DIMOND

ABOVE: G2u No. 2660, like most of the CPR's G2 Pacifics, was modernized during the 1920s; while some classmates received a new boiler, new cylinders, and even a new frame, larger (22.5x28") cylinders were the extent of modifications made at the time to this and 107 other G2 engines. ROBERT F. COLLINS, MORNING SUN BOOKS COLLECTION

BELOW: N2b Consolidation No. 3725 was built by MLW in 1912 as N3b No. 3925, and renumbered in January 1927. At McAdam on March 3, 1960, it was nearing the end of a 48-year career. ROBERT F. COLLINS, MORNING SUN BOOKS COLLECTION

RIGHT: Given the date—March 3, 1960—this gathering of locomotives under steam, without a diesel in sight, was truly remarkable. Awaiting their next—and among their last—assignments at the McAdam engine terminal were semi-streamlined F1a 4-4-4 Jubilee No. 2926, N2b 2-8-0 No. 3725, and, looking a bit the worse for wear, V4a 0-8-0 switcher No. 6941. ROBERT F. COLLINS, MORNING SUN BOOKS COLLECTION

OPPOSITE BOTTOM: Canadian Pacific embraced the Budd RDC as a means of trimming deficits on its branchline and secondary schedules, eventually rostering 55 units. Operating in McAdam–Saint John service, RDC-4 No. 9200 was being worked on the north side of McAdam station on August 17, 1956, prior to departing with RDC-2 No. 9102 as Train No. 153 for Saint John Union Station. GEORGE DIMOND

Its junction location dictated by railway route requirements rather than proximity to any population center, the CPR's remote McAdam, N.B., station incorporated a main-floor restaurant and second-floor hotel for the benefit of passengers making connections or otherwise laying over between trains. Built in 1910, the structure survives and has been accorded protected landmark status. On August 1, 1959, F1a Jubilee No. 2926 trundled past the station with Train No. 562. Passenger accommodations on the train to St. Andrews and St. Stephen had been eliminated in favor of SMT bus service; CPR tickets were honored on the buses, but a timetable note indicated that "heavy checked baggage will be handled in wayfreight service."
ROBERT F. COLLINS, MORNING SUN BOOKS COLLECTION

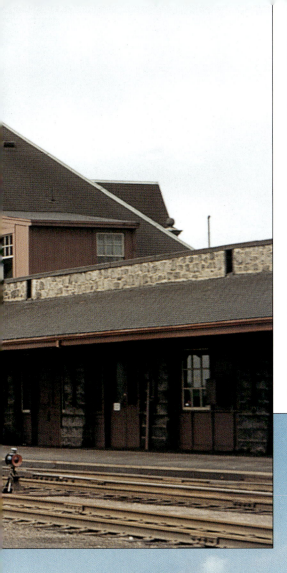

ABOVE: F1a Jubilee No. 2928 hustled away from Watt, N.B., on Sept. 5, 1957, leading mixed train M564 over its 42-mile trip between McAdam and St. Andrews.

At Watt, the line from McAdam split into two branches; one reaching St. Stephen on the U.S-Canada border, and the other terminating at the Bay of Fundy resort and fishing community of St. Andrews. On Sept. 5, 1957, Jubilee No. 2928 switched freight cars using the line to St. Stephen before continuing south with M564 to St. Andrews on the track visible behind the station. BOTH, GEORGE DIMOND

TOP: Gas-electric No. 9008 was operating as McAdam–St. Stephen Train No. 122 when it paused at Watt on September 5, 1957. The schedule allowed one hour and ten minutes for the 34-mile run. GEORGE DIMOND

MIDDLE: Arriving at Watt 20 minutes after Train No. 122, mixed M564 had several freight cars to pick up on Sept. 5, 1957, before proceeding to St. Andrews. GEORGE DIMOND

BELOW: The CPR's compact yard and station area in St. Stephen lay beside the St. Croix River, with the Maine Central's small terminal in Calais, Me., visible across the waterway. In this circa-1956 scene, Jubilee No. 2928 will soon depart for Watt and McAdam with Train No. 151. The roof of the CPR station is just visible above No. 2928's tender. PRESTON JOHNSON

TOP: Although something of an incongruity—with their semi-streamlining, 75-inch drivers, and "passenger" livery—the CPR's F1a Jubilees were nonetheless intended for light-duty wayfreight operations precisely like those being handled by No. 2926 at St. Andrews on July 31, 1959.

MIDDLE: No. 2926 worked the St. Andrews fish pier at low tide on the same day.

LEFT: The Bay of Fundy's remarkable tides are evident in this high-tide view on March 3, 1960. ALL, ROBERT F. COLLINS, MORNING SUN BOOKS COLLECTION

If the semi-streamlined Jubilees employed by the CPR in its New Brunswick operations embodied the modern end of the steam spectrum, then the opposite extreme could be found only a few miles away—and as late as 1960, as well—in the antiquated locomotives and infrastructure of the Minto Subdivision. Light bridge loadings dictated that a handful of 4-4-0s be kept in operation between Chipman and Norton, N.B., until suitably light diesels could be acquired. On April 25, 1959, class A1e No. 29 was coaled the hard way at Chipman. ROBERT F. COLLINS, MORNING SUN BOOKS COLLECTION

The three 4-4-0s that closed out the steam era on the Minto Subdivision were not as old as they looked. While their frames and other durable portions of the engines were original and dated to the earliest years of the CPR's existence, the trio had been rebuilt so thoroughly over the ensuing decades that the "sum of the parts" was not as easily dated. Regardless of their age, these last 4-4-0s in North American mainline service had garnered celebrity status long before their final runs; fans and photographers made regular pilgrimages to record the CPR's New Brunswick "time machine." On April 25, 1959, Nos. 29 and 144 were the objects of attention at Chipman. ROBERT F. COLLINS, MORNING SUN BOOKS COLLECTION

No. 29 started its career in September 1887, built by the CPR's Montreal shops as Class SA No. 390. In March 1893 it returned to the shops, where among other improvements its original 62-inch drivers were replaced by larger 69-inch versions. At that time it was reclassified as SC, but still retained its original number. In March 1908 it was reclassed and renumbered as A6a No. 217, receiving 70-inch drivers, and in August 1913 it received its final classification and road number during a thorough rebuild. Other elements of the engine's transformation, in common with its latter-day rostermates, included replacement or rebuilding of the boiler, firebox, cab, tender, headlight, numberplate, and pilot. In these two 1959 views, the spit-and-polish 4-4-0 simmers at the Chipman, N.B., engine terminal. RIGHT, ROBERT F. COLLINS, MORNING SUN BOOKS COLLECTION; BELOW, GEORGE DIMOND

THIS PAGE AND OPPOSITE TOP: In a ritual that endured for almost a year after these images were recorded on April 25, 1959, class A1e No. 29 was readied at Chipman for its next trip down the Minto Subdivision to Norton, 44.6 miles distant. In addition to modest on-line traffic, the route served as a link between the CNR's Moncton–Saint John and Moncton–Edmunston main lines. ALL, ROBERT F. COLLINS, MORNING SUN BOOKS COLLECTION

OPPOSITE MIDDLE: Several years earlier, No. 29 was tended to beside the Chipman enginehouse. PRESTON JOHNSON

OPPOSITE BOTTOM: Class A2q 4-4-0 No. 144, with its smokebox freshly painted, rested on one of the Chipman enginehouse leads in April 1959. ROBERT F. COLLINS, MORNING SUN BOOKS COLLECTION

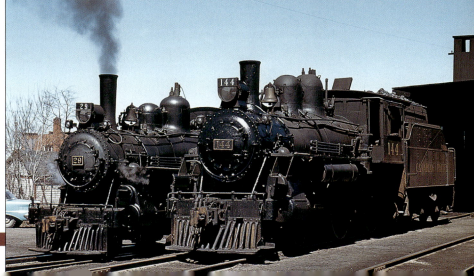

ABOVE: Class A2q No. 144's final incarnation dated to January 1914, when it was rebuilt from class A7a No. 230, in the process gaining drivers one inch larger than its former 62-inch editions. It traced its lineage to the CPR's Montreal shops, where it was delivered in March 1886 as class SA No. 351, being rebuilt into No. 230 in December 1907. In its final guise, the 4-4-0 had seen some recent paintwork at Chipman on April 25, 1959. ROBERT F. COLLINS, MORNING SUN BOOKS COLLECTION

MIDDLE: Nos. 29 and 144 rubbed shoulders at Chipman circa 1954. PRESTON JOHNSON

BOTTOM: Class A2m No. 136 was the oldest member of the Minto Subdivision's celebrity trio, as far as original construction dates went. A Rogers product of August 1883 (No. 140), it became A5h No. 196 in May 1907; A5h No. 115 in Sept. 1912; and its final identity of No. 136 in August 1913. AUTHOR'S COLLECTION

OPPOSITE Modernity and antiquity were juxtaposed at Chipman on March 5, 1960. The recently assigned CLC diesel had balked, and No. 29 was pressed into passenger service for one final week. BOTH, ROBERT F. COLLINS, MORNING SUN BOOKS COLLECTION

ABOVE AND RIGHT: On August 17, 1956, A2q No. 144 led mixed M160 at Pennlyn, N.B., the first station south of Chipman on the way to Norton. Two hours and 20 minutes were allotted for the 47.4-mile trip. BOTH, GEORGE DIMOND

Passengers passed the time between Chipman and Norton aboard CPR combine No. 3361, shown in these two views at Pennlyn on October 8, 1959. BOTH, ROBERT F. COLLINS, MORNING SUN BOOKS COLLECTION

By 1959, Canadian Pacific's Chipman–Norton mixed trains had been renumbered from M159 and M160 to M559 and M560, and in the fall of 1959 the night terminal was changed from Norton to Chipman. On April 25, 1959, A1e No. 29 led M560 across the bridge at Pennlyn. This recently rebuilt span had been one of three responsible for the weight restrictions that saw the trio of 4-4-0s survive in Minto Sub. operations until 1960. Their remaining duties were assumed in October 1959 by a variation of the 44-ton diesel popularized by General Electric, built, in the CPR's case, by CLC in Kingston, Ontario; diesel-hydraulic No. 18 (classed an HS-5d by the CPR) was sent east from its original assignment in Ontario, relegating the 4-4-0s to backup status. BOTH, ROBERT F. COLLINS, MORNING SUN BOOKS COLLECTION

ABOVE: No. 144 approached Granville, N.B., on August 17, 1956, with the Norton-bound mixed train. When this engine's flues expired in the fall of 1959, its return to Montreal for preservation left Nos. 29 and 136 to face the imminent arrival of diesels on the Minto Subdivision. GEORGE DIMOND

BELOW: In the first week of March 1960 the CLC diesel assigned to Chipman failed, and No. 29 had one last fling in regular service (No. 136 had been given a similar send-off that January). On March 5, the veteran 4-4-0 called at Cumberland Bay, N.B., with M560. ROBERT F. COLLINS, MORNING SUN BOOKS COLLECTION

ABOVE: Three years before its retirement, No. 144 paused with M160 at Young's Cove Road, N.B., on August 17, 1956. Following a brief foray in excursion service in November 1959, this locomotive was donated to the Canadian Railway Historical Association and placed on display at the Canadian Railway Museum in Delson-St. Constant, Quebec. GEORGE DIMOND

RIGHT: On April 25, 1959, No. 29 ambled near Cody with M560. The train has just crossed another of the line's restrictive bridges, a moveable span across an inlet of Washademoak Lake. ROBERT F. COLLINS, MORNING SUN BOOKS COLLECTION

OPPOSITE: Farther along in its journey to Norton, M560 crossed this composite trestle north of Belleisle on April 25, 1959. ROBERT F. COLLINS, MORNING SUN BOOKS COLLECTION

Traversing open country in the last few miles of its run, M560's locomotive, combine, and crew would tie up for the night in Norton, four miles ahead (until the mixed train's schedule was reversed in October 1959). The short train in these April 25, 1959, views betrayed the line's light traffic and uncertain future, although excursionists occasionally doubled the mixed's passenger car count as railfan groups opted to ride behind North America's last 4-4-0s in regular service. Not surprisingly, given their notoriety, all three engines were preserved, seeing individual excursion service and even a fleeting television career following retirement.
ALL, ROBERT F. COLLINS, MORNING SUN BOOKS COLLECTION

ABOVE: Coming into Norton across the Kennebecasis River on April 25, 1959, Train M560 negotiated the the third of three bridges responsible for the 4-4-0s' longevity on this line. This span had a four m.p.h. slow order, just to be safe.

LEFT: No. 29, at the end of its run to Norton on April 25, 1959.

RIGHT: Earlier the same day, Chipman-bound M559 awaited its morning departure from Norton, where the CPR shared facilites on Canadian National's former Intercolonial route between Moncton and Saint John. ALL, ROBERT F. COLLINS, MORNING SUN BOOKS COLLECTION

ABOVE AND OPPOSITE TOP: No. 29 was ready to leave Norton with M559 on April 25, 1959, for the two hour and 50 minute run to Chipman. The 4-4-0's patchwork heritage is evident, at a glance, from its mismatched pilot-truck wheels. To No. 29 went the bittersweet honor, on November 6, 1960, of leading what was then billed as the last official steam-powered train on the Canadian Pacific. In retirement, and a long way from Norton, following the company's corporate move from Montreal in the mid-1990s No. 29 was given pride of place on display at the entrance to Canadian Pacific's new Calgary, Alberta, headquarters. In its wake, the railway saw fit in the late 1990s to repatriate, restore, and return to operation H1b Hudson No. 2816 for business-train and public relations assignments. ALL, ROBERT F. COLLINS, MORNING SUN BOOKS COLLECTION

BELOW: Flange-wheeled track inspection automobile M296 was touring the Minto Subdivision at Norton circa 1953. PRESTON JOHNSON

ABOVE: No. 29 was at North Devon, N.B., circa 1954. Passengers reached the provincial capital of Fredericton from here via a short SMT bus connection. PRESTON JOHNSON

RIGHT: At Kilburn, N.B., on March 4, 1960, an RDC-3/RDC-4 duo running as McAdam–Edmunston Train No. 123 met G2e Pacific No. 2644 on southbound First 84.

BELOW: No. 2644 crossed the Saint John River at Perth, en route to McAdam on March 4, 1960. BOTH, ROBERT F. COLLINS, MORNING SUN BOOKS COLLECTION

LEFT: On February 10, 1950, D4g No. 491 (Angus Shops, 1914) awaited its departure from Edmunston with Train No. 154 for McAdam.

BELOW: Class G2u No. 2644 was delivered by MLW in June 1913 as G2e No. 1244. Rebuilt with one-inch-larger drivers (from 69" to 70") and renumbered in May 1914, the Pacific was further rebuilt and reclassified in mid-1928. With green flags snapping, it led First 84 south at Aroostook, N.B., on March 4, 1960. By April 14, when D10j No. 986 tied up in McAdam, steam's curtain had fallen in New Brunswick. BOTH, ROBERT F. COLLINS, MORNING SUN BOOKS COLLECTION

QUEBEC
La Belle Province

On the south shore of the St. Lawrence River but well within Montreal's urban orbit, Adirondack Junction, at the south end of the CPR's river crossing, marked the intersection of the railway's Adirondack Subdivision with a border-hopping New York Central route to Syracuse, New York. On May 9, 1959, G2s Pacific No. 2541 led a 30-car wayfreight through the junction. In just under a year, all Canadian Pacific Railway operations would be dieselized.
ROBERT F. COLLINS, MORNING SUN BOOKS COLLECTION

Canadian Pacific's home province for more than a century, Quebec presented observers of the CPR with a remarkable diversity ranging from isolated rural branch lines and remote secondary routes to some of the busiest urban mainline trackage in Canada. American carriers Delaware & Hudson and New York Central added more variety to the mix by employing CPR trackage rights to reach Montreal.

Leased by the CPR in 1912, the Quebec Central Railway endured as a separate entity, for legal reasons, beyond the end of the steam era, although after the fires died in early 1960 motive power no longer wore QC lettering. Quebec Central operations encompassed those routes forming a triangle south of the St. Lawrence River to connect Sherbrooke and Mégantic with the Quebec City area via Vallée Jonction (Valley Junction) and Tring Junction.

With the railway's operations firmly anchored in Montreal, CPR main lines radiated from there to Ottawa and the West; to Toronto and vital U.S. connections in southern Ontario; to Quebec City via the St. Lawrence's north shore; and to Sherbrooke and connections with both the Quebec Central and, beyond, to the International of Maine. South of the Montreal–Sherbrooke main, two other important routes headed south to the U.S. border. The Napierville Junction Railway linked its parent Delaware & Hudson with the CPR, while Canadian Pacific achieved its own New England access via Newport, St. Johnsbury, and Wells River, Vermont.

TOP: Lowelltown, Maine, was the westernmost U.S. station on the CPR's International of Maine Division; it was 3.8 miles east of the aptly named Boundary, Quebec. Class G2s Pacific No. 2584 led the "Scoot" at Lowelltown. on February 25, 1956.

MIDDLE: Mégantic, Quebec, 15 miles west of the international border, saw some of "the old ways" persist through the 1950s even beyond the coal-smoke-scented confines of the CPR yard. The cultural contrasts—as in this January 3, 1959 view—were not lost on American rail enthusiasts visiting the region.

BELOW: Mégantic was the western terminus of the "Scoots," the mixed trains serving locales along the International of Maine to Brownville Junction. G2s Pacific No. 2584 was in charge of eastbound M118 on February 25, 1956, awaiting the morning's departure from Mégantic. ALL, ROBERT F. COLLINS, MORNING SUN BOOKS COLLECTION

Class G2s Pacific No. 2583 was switching at the east end of Mégantic's yard on October 6, 1958, prior to leading a train to Brownville Junction, Maine.
GEORGE DIMOND; TIMETABLE AND UNIFORM BUTTON, AUTHOR'S COLLECTION

CANADIAN PACIFIC RAILWAY
EASTERN REGION–QUEBEC DISTRICT
EXCEPT MONTREAL TERMINALS

TIME 34 TABLE

TAKING EFFECT at 12.01 a.m., SUNDAY, OCTOBER 29th, 1950
GOVERNED BY EASTERN STANDARD TIME
FOR THE INFORMATION AND GUIDANCE OF EMPLOYEES ONLY

THE SUPERIOR DIRECTION IS EAST OR SOUTH, AND EAST OR SOUTH BOUND TRAINS ARE SUPERIOR TO TRAINS OF THE SAME CLASS IN THE OPPOSITE (INFERIOR) DIRECTION

THE COMPANY'S RULES ARE PRINTED SEPARATELY IN BOOK FORM. EVERY EMPLOYEE WHOSE DUTIES ARE PRESCRIBED BY THE RULES AND EVERY EMPLOYEE WHOSE DUTIES ARE CONNECTED WITH THE MOVEMENT OF TRAINS, MUST HAVE A COPY OF THE RULES AND OF THE CURRENT TIME TABLE ACCESSIBLE WHEN ON DUTY

G. N. CURLEY,
GENERAL MANAGER

F. A. POULIOT,
GENERAL SUPERINTENDENT

LEFT AND MIDDLE: Bound for the asbestos mining center of Thetford Mines, on the Quebec Central's line to Sherbrooke, CPR class D10k 4-6-0 No. 1066 departs Vallée Jonction (Valley Junction) on January 3, 1959. Boasting the world's largest concentration of asbestos production, Thetford Mines grew steadily after the Quebec Central linked the area with ocean shipping at Levis. BOTH, GEORGE DIMOND

BOTTOM LEFT: Class G2s Pacific No. 2541 hustled Train No. 24 through the snow near Vallée Jonction on March 1, 1960. ROBERT F. COLLINS, MORNING SUN BOOKS COLLECTION

RIGHT: Leased by the CPR to Quebec Central and lettered accordingly, D10g No. 890 trundled through Vallée Jonction on July 9, 1959. GEORGE DIMOND

BELOW RIGHT: Also lettered for Quebec Central, D10g No. 871 prepared to depart Vallée Jonction on October 6, 1959. ROBERT F. COLLINS, MORNING SUN BOOKS COLLECTION

OPPOSITE: **Behind leased and relettered CPR G2s Pacific No. 2556, Quebec Central mixed No. 24 has just left Vallée Jonction on October 6, 1959, and faces a 12-mile climb through rolling farmland to Summit.** BOTH, ROBERT F. COLLINS, MORNING SUN BOOKS COLLECTION

RIGHT: **CPR G2u No. 2663 works upgrade out of Vallée Jonction on July 9, 1959, with a freight bound for Thetford Mines.** GEORGE DIMOND

BELOW: **The Quebec Central's Vallée Jonction–Mégantic mixed train No. 24 follows the Chaudière River out of Vallée Jonction on July 9, 1959. This day's run was led by G2s No. 2554, just out of sight around the curve. At Tring Junction, the train will leave the QC's Sherbrooke line and strike south to Mégantic.** GEORGE DIMOND

RIGHT: On July 7, 1959, Quebec Central D10g No. 871 shared the Vallée Jonction engine terminal with five-year-old RS-3 No. 8450. GEORGE DIMOND

BELOW LEFT: Well-manicured No. 871 was a 1910 product of the CPR's Angus Shops. ROBERT F. COLLINS, MORNING SUN BOOKS COLLECTION

BELOW RIGHT: A March 1, 1960, visit inside the Vallée Jonction enginehouse found D10e No. 814 being preened. The CPR had a total of 495 D10 class 4-6-0 locomotives in service at the end of World War II, making dieselization a protracted process. ROBERT F. COLLINS, MORNING SUN BOOKS COLLECTION

A total of 14 diesel-hydraulic locomotives helped the CPR address the lightweight end of the dieselization spectrum. Built by CLC between 1957 and 1960, the units pushed steam from a number of branchline terminals; No. 23 was at Vallée Jonction in July 1961. GEORGE DIMOND

ABOVE: Budd Rail Diesel Cars—dubbed "Dayliners" on the CPR—found a home on the Quebec Central after 1957; unlike a pair assigned to the Dominion Atlantic, however, RDC's used on the QC all wore regular CANADIAN PACIFIC lettering. On January 3, 1959, Quebec Central Train No. 1, the daily Sherbrooke–Quebec City service, crossed the Chaudiere River to the expectant stares of passengers boarding at Vallée Jonction. Its station work complete, the train promptly continued north. Nose-door mounted portable Pyle Gyralites were a hallmark of the CPR's Dayliner fleet. BOTH, GEORGE DIMOND

BELOW: On March 1, 1960, the Dayliner serving as QC Train No. 1 breezed past a freight train led by D10k No. 1083 at Scotts Junction. ROBERT F. COLLINS, MORNING SUN BOOKS COLLECTION

An appendage of the Quebec Central ran 78.5 miles from Vallée Jonction to Lac Frontière, a rural outpost on the Quebec-Maine international border almost due east of Quebec City. Daily-except-Sunday service over the Chaudière Subdivision was provided by mixed trains Nos. 34 and 35, counterparts to the pair of mixeds (Nos. 24 and 25) operating on the Mégantic Subdivision between Vallée Jonction and Mégantic. The first station east of Vallée Jonction on the line to Lac Frontière was St. Joseph, where G2t Pacific No. 2609 led a healthy No. 35 on the last leg of its scheduled five hour and 45 minute trip from Lac Frontière on October 6, 1959.
ROBERT F. COLLINS, MORNING SUN BOOKS COLLECTION

QUEBEC CENTRAL PUBLIC TIMETABLE, OCT. 1957; AUTHOR'S COLLECTION

QUEBEC—SHERBROOKE

Read Down—Lire de haut en bas   Read Up—Lire de bas en haut

♥4 Daily Quotidien P.M.	♥2 Except Sunday Dim. excepté A.M.	Miles	←TRAIN No.→ TABLE TABLEAU 1	♥1 Daily Quotidien P.M.	♥3 Daily Quotidien P.M.
3 50	6 30		Dep **Quebec** (Palais St'n)..Ar	2 15	11 35
4 18	7 03	14.2	" Charny (QC-CN)....Dep	1 45	11 05
f4 31	f7 16	20.4	" Breakeyville......... "	f1 32	f10 52
f4 38	f7 23	26.1	" Ville Lambert........ "	f1 25	f10 45
f4 44	f7 29	30.4	" Bras.................. "	f1 19	f10 39
4 52	7 36	36.1	" Scotts Jct.............. "	1 11	10 31
4 59	7 42	40.9	" Ste. Marie............ "	1 04	10 24
5 08	7 51	47.8	Ar **Vallee Jct.**........ Dep	12 55	10 15
				12 42	10 02
5 22	8 05	57.3	Dep **Tring Jct.**........ Ar	12 34	9 54
5 30	8 13	62.9	" East Broughton...... Dep	f12 26	f9 46
f5 38	f8 21	68.1	" Leeds................. "	f12 19	f9 39
f5 45	f8 28	73.0	" Robertson............ "	12 14	9 34
5 50	8 33	76.9	" Thetford Mines...... "	12 05	9 25
5 59	8 42	84.2	" Black Lake........... "	f11 57	f9 17
f6 07	f8 50	90.0	" Coleraine............. "	11 50	9 10
6 14	8 57	94.9	" Disraeli............... "	f11 43	f9 03
f6 21	f9 04	100.1	" Garthby............... "	f11 35	f8 55
f6 29	f9 12	106.1	" St. Gerard............ "	f11 29	f8 49
f6 35	f9 18	110.8	" Weedon............... "	f11 15	f8 35
f6 50	f9 32	121.3	" Bishopton............ "	10 59	8 19
7 06	9 48	130.7	" East Angus........... "	f10 47	f8 07
f7 18	f9 59	137.1	" Ascot................. "	10 30	7 50
7 35	10 15	147.6	Ar **Sherbrooke** (QC-CP Station) Dep	A.M.	P.M.
P.M.	A.M.				

Makes direct connections from Montreal—Fait le raccordement direct pour Montréal

EXPLANATION OF SIGNS
♥ Air-condition Rail Diesel car. No baggage checked.
m Mixed train—Coaches.
f Flag stop.
Note—Train No. 24 will operate Mon., Wed. and Fri. only Oct. 27 to Dec. 14 inc., April 6 to April 26 inc. Train No. 25 will operate Tues., Thurs. and Sat. only Oct. 27 to Dec. 14 inc., April 6 to April 26 inc.

RENVOIS
♥ Autorail diesel climatisé. Il n'y a pas d'enregistrement de bagage.
m Trains mixtes—Voitures.
f Arrêt sur signal.
Note—Le train No 24 opérera lundi, mer. et ven. seulement 27 oct. au 14 déc. inc., 6 avril au 26 avril inc. Le train No 25 opérera mardi, jeudi et sam. seulement 27 oct. au 14 déc. inc., 6 avril au 26 avril inc.

VALLEE JCT.—LAC FRONTIERE

Read Down—Lire de haut en bas   Read Up—Lire de bas en haut

34m Except Sunday Dim. excepté P.M.	Miles	←TRAIN No.→ TABLE TABLEAU 2	35m Except Sunday Dim. excepté P.M.
5 40		Dep **Vallee Jct.**........ Ar	2 15
6 00	4.8	" St. Joseph............Dep	2 03
6 30	14.5	" Beauceville........... "	1 35
f6 40	18.6	" Notre Dame des Pins.. "	f1 10
7 05	22.8	" St. Georges........... "	1 00
f7 25	28.4	" Cumberland.......... "	f12 35
8 00	34.8	" Morisset.............. "	12 15
8 25	41.3	" Ste. Rose............. "	11 45
8 45	45.1	" Ste. Germaine........ "	11 10
9 15	50.6	" Ste. Justine........... "	10 40
9 40	54.8	" Ste. Sabine........... "	9 50
10 05	60.2	" St. Camille............ "	9 35
f10 25	68.0	" St. Just............... "	f9 01
10 35	70.1	" Daaquam............. "	8 55
10 55	78.5	Ar **Lac Frontiere**......Dep	8 30
P.M.			A.M.

VALLEE JCT.—TRING JCT.—MEGANTIC

Read Down—Lire de haut en bas   Read Up—Lire de bas en haut

24m Daily Quotidien P.M.	Miles	←TRAIN No.→ TABLE TABLEAU 3	25m Daily Quotidien A.M.
......		Dep **Vallee Jct.**........ Ar	8 35
......	9.5	Ar **Tring Jct.**..........Dep	8 10
5 25		Dep **Tring Jct.**......... Ar	7 45
f5 36	13.9	" St. Jules.............. "	f7 34
5 50	19.4	" St. Victor............. "	7 20
6 06	25.7	" St. Ephrem........... "	7 04
6 25	33.4	" St. Evariste........... "	6 45
6 50	41.5	" Courcelles............ "	6 25
7 20	50.2	" St. Sebastien......... "	6 02
7 35	55.3	" St. Samuel........... "	5 49
f7 45	58.5	" Ste. Cecile........... "	f5 40
8 15	68.4	Ar **Megantic** (QC-CP)..Dep	5 15
P.M.			A.M.

(See—Voir Note)

LEFT: Traveling through Beauceville, 14.5 miles out of Vallée Jonction, D10j No. 970 led mixed train No. 35 from Lac Frontière along the bank of the Chaudière River on October 5, 1959. This 4-6-0 had been built by MLW in September 1912.

ABOVE: G2t Pacific No. 2609 paused with mixed No. 35 on October 6, 1959, at Morriset, just over halfway through the day's trip to Vallée Jonction. Reclassified from a G2e when it received smaller cylinders in 1928 (going from 22.5x28 to 20x28 inches), No. 2609 was built by Angus Shops in March 1912 as G2e No. 1209, receiving its later number as part of a January 1914 shopping that also saw its driver diameter increased from 69 to 70 inches. Scrapping came in January 1961.

BOTH, ROBERT F. COLLINS, MORNING SUN BOOKS COLLECTION

ABOVE: Train No. 35 arrives at Morriset on October 6, 1959.

Earlier that day at Daaquam, G2t Pacific No. 2609 was only 8.4 miles into its trip from Lac Frontière to Vallée Jonction as it lifted cars of pulpwood from the town's team track.
BOTH, ROBERT F. COLLINS, MORNING SUN BOOKS COLLECTION

LEFT: Its work complete, No. 2609 led its train out of Daaquam on October 6, 1959.

BELOW: Thirty-three miles from Lac Frontière, No. 2609 led Quebec Central mixed No. 35 into St. Germaine, having picked up a couple of tank cars since leaving Daaquam.
BOTH, ROBERT F. COLLINS, MORNING SUN BOOKS COLLECTION

In this trio of views taken at Scotts Junction, Quebec, on March 1, 1960, D10k No. 1074—an Alco Schenectady product of 1912—eases its wayfreight past the enclosed and heated octagonal water tank. A short time before, the 4-6-0 had met sister D10k No. 1083, the latter leased to Quebec Central and wearing QC lettering. CPR steam had just weeks left, and when the end finally came for these engines it was swift; No. 1083 was scrapped in August 1960, and No. 1074 followed it to the torch that December. As much hallmarks of Canadian railroading as the enclosed tank were the pair of wooden high-cupola CPR "vans" (cabooses) awaiting their next assignments. Scotts Junction was the point at which Quebec Central routes to Lévis and Quebec City (on the south and north shores of the St. Lawrence, respectively) met; to reach either of these endpoints, however, QC trains had to travel over Canadian National rails for the final few miles.

ALL, ROBERT F. COLLINS,
MORNING SUN BOOKS COLLECTION;
UNIFORM BUTTON, AUTHOR'S COLLECTION

Before Budd RDC's took over (see page 67), conventional CPR passenger equipment was assigned to the Quebec Central's Sherbrooke–Vallée Jonction–Quebec City schedules. On August 12, 1956, G2u No. 2610 led QC's Train No. 1 through Bishopton, 26.3 miles east of Sherbrooke. On the head end was mail-and-express car No. 3606, built in the distinctive curved-side style favored by CPR motive power and rolling stock chief H.B. Bowen in the years immediately before and after World War II. BOTH, ROBERT F. COLLINS, MORNING SUN BOOKS COLLECTION

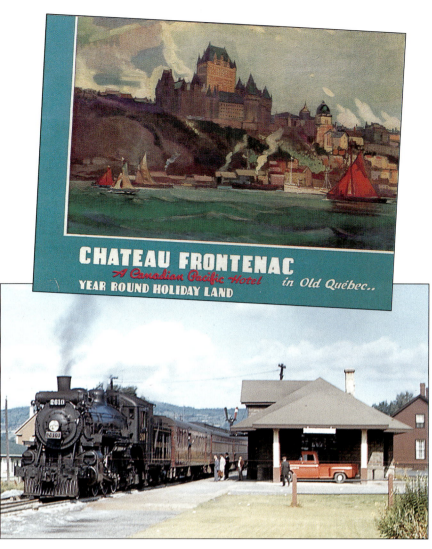

ABOVE: QC Train No. 1 paused at East Angus, Quebec, on August 12, 1956.

BELOW: No. 2610 leads the QC's modest flagship train through Ascot Corners, early in its 147.6-mile Sherbrooke–Quebec City run on August 12, 1956. Upon reaching the environs of Quebec's provincial capital—site of the CPR's famous Chateau Frontenac hotel—QC trains employed CNR trackage rights to cross the St. Lawrence via the landmark Quebec Bridge and reach jointly-operated Palais Station.
BOTH, ROBERT F. COLLINS, MORNING SUN BOOKS COLLECTION; BROCHURE, AUTHOR'S COLLECTION

At Johnville, Quebec, 10.3 miles east of Sherbrooke on the Mégantic Subdivision, burly double-headed Mikados led a reefer-heavy eastbound freight toward Mégantic on August 12, 1956. In the lead was P2f No. 5399, built by MLW in November 1928; in second position was P2c No. 5333, an MLW product of October 1923. Despite their relative youth, both 2-8-2s had only one year's service left; they were scrapped in August 1957.
BOTH, ROBERT F. COLLINS, MORNING SUN BOOKS COLLECTION

Farther west on the Mégantic Subdivision, barely four miles out of the division point of Sherbrooke, the two P2 Mikados led their eastbound 31-car train out of Lennoxville on August 12, 1956. At this point in their trip, trailing P2c No. 5333 appears to be working harder than P2f No. 5399 up front. BOTH, ROBERT F. COLLINS, MORNING SUN BOOKS COLLECTION

LEFT: Class P2g Mikado No. 5406 led a 16-car eastbound extra through Lennoxville on August 11, 1956. This locomotive was the second of a batch of 12 "war babies" built by MLW in 1940; they were the first new CPR Mikados since the P2f's of 1928. ROBERT F. COLLINS, MORNING SUN BOOKS COLLECTION

BELOW: September 4, 1956 found P1e Mikado No. 5194 (formerly P1b No. 5094, built by MLW in October 1913) and D10k No. 1068 (Alco Schenectady, October 1912) at Sherbrooke. PRESTON JOHNSON

ABOVE: On a sultry August 11, 1956, P2g Mikado No. 5410 and P2h sibling No. 5421 led a westbound freight at Sherbrooke.

BELOW: More doubleheaded power, with P2j Mikado No. 5458 trailing, eastbound at Sherbrooke on February 24, 1956.

RIGHT: Quebec Central Train No. 1 departed Sherbrooke behind G2u Pacific No. 2610 on August 12, 1956. The four-car Sherbrooke–Quebec City consist included an express-mail car, coaches, and a buffet-restaurant car. South of Sherbrooke, a Quebec Central bus to and from Newport, Vermont, provided hardy travelers with connections to the CPR-Boston & Maine schedules reaching Boston and New York.

OPPOSITE BOTTOM: Class P2f Mikado No. 5399, MLW class of 1928, took on water at Sherbrooke before leading an eastbound freight to Mégantic. ALL, ROBERT F. COLLINS, MORNING SUN BOOKS COLLECTION

OPPOSITE: G2u Pacific No. 2610 will soon depart Sherbrooke station with QC Train No. 1 for Quebec City on August 12, 1956, not long before the run was converted to Budd RDC "Dayliners." Behind steam power, No. 1 was allowed five hours and 10 minutes for the 147.6-mile run.

RIGHT: Class D10f No. 847, at Sherbrooke on August 11, 1956, was a study in functional simplicity. Built by MLW in October 1909 as No. 2647, the 4-6-0 was renumbered in February 1913, and scrapped in January 1959.

BELOW: Later that day, No. 847 was lent a helping hand leading its 20 cars out of Sherbrooke by S-2 No. 7026.
ALL, ROBERT F. COLLINS, MORNING SUN BOOKS COLLECTION

85

ABOVE: Leased to the Quebec Central, D10k No. 1072 was working at Sherbrooke on "Leap Day," February 29, 1960. The 4-6-0 entered CPR service in October 1912 upon its delivery from Alco's Schenectady works. Its career spanned almost a half-century, before retirement and scrapping in May 1961. ROBERT F. COLLINS, MORNING SUN BOOKS COLLECTION

BELOW AND RIGHT: West of its namesake, the Sherbrooke Subdivision traversed the northern reaches of the Appalachian range. Near Mont Orford on April 16, 1960, with the last snow not yet melted from the shadows, the RDC "Dayliners" of weekend-only Train No. 204 passed through on their way from Montreal's Windsor Station to Sherbrooke. The day's main attraction, however, soon appeared in the form of G5a Pacific No. 1201 leading a Canadian Railway Historical Association excursion. This Pacific's status as the last new steam engine built by the CPR (in June 1944) made it a favored fan-trip engine as the railway's steam era passed.
BOTH, ROBERT F. COLLINS, MORNING SUN BOOKS COLLECTION

OPPOSITE TOP: In his 1944 G5 design, CPR motive power chief Henry Bowen melded modern materials and construction techniques with the proven (if somewhat obsolescent) 4-6-2 wheel arrangement. His goal was to create a "new" locomotive, based on the railway's earlier G2 class, that would be nimble enough for service throughout the CPR system as a replacement for older G1 and G2 Pacifics and D10 4-6-0s; even in 1944, Bowen—ever the steam stalwart—did not consider diesels to be a suitable option. Along with classmate No. 1200, delivered in April 1944, the two G5a's were the first locomotives to be built at the CPR's Angus Shops since 1931. They were also the last. No. 1201 posed at Farnham, Quebec, on April 16, 1960.

LEFT AND BELOW: Stylistically, Bowen is best remembered for his sloping, "moon-faced" front-end treatments (so characterized by *Trains* magazine's late editor, David P. Morgan), in both standard and semi-streamlined variations. Class P2g Mikado No. 5406 exhibited the Bowen "look" at Foster (left) and Farnham in August 1956.

ABOVE: Class P2j Mikado No. 5447 (MLW, June 1944), at Farnham on August 12, 1956, showed the typical striping and lettering arrangement applied to the P2 class.
ALL, ROBERT F. COLLINS, MORNING SUN BOOKS COLLECTION

OPPOSITE TOP: Class D10g No. 946 eased past the Farnham station with a short wayfreight on February 29, 1960. Scrapped just over a year later, in May 1961, the 4-6-0 was built by MLW in October 1911 as CPR No. 2746. The CPR favored rather austere architecture for its postwar structures, and the two-story Farnham Division office building was a typical example.

LEFT AND ABOVE: Freshly wiped down, P2g Mikado No. 5406 strode out of Farnham with an eastbound extra on August 11, 1956. ALL, ROBERT F. COLLINS, MORNING SUN BOOKS COLLECTION; TICKET ENVELOPE, AUTHOR'S COLLECTION

Canadian Pacific's D4g class of light 4-6-0s had a reputation for being rough-riding, difficult-to-fire locomotives, but that didn't stop one of their number from achieving a brief career as an excursion leader at steam's twilight. Although among the lowest-numbered of the D4g's, No. 424 was the youngest of the class, built at the railway's Angus Shops in May 1915. The 75 D4g's were intended to go where the CPR's heavier D10 4-6-0s could not; Angus turned out 49 of the stubby but slender design, with MLW contributing the rest. At Farnham on October 3, 1959, No. 424 and trailing D10g No. 946 were buffed to a high shine for their day's assignment to a CRHA excursion.

BOTH, ROBERT F. COLLINS, MORNING SUN BOOKS COLLECTION

TOP: Class G5c Pacific No. 1258 occupied the turntable at Grand-Mère on May 28, 1957. This was one of 100 G5 Pacifics built for the CPR by MLW and CLC *after* World War II, as Bowen still refused to embrace dieselization beyond yard limits. GEORGE DIMOND

MIDDLE: Retrieved from its erstwhile New Brunswick home, venerable A1e 4-4-0 No. 29 contrasted with its sleek excursion consist of three smooth-sided lightweight cars at Ste. Thérèse on November 6, 1960. The occasion: the last official run of Canadian Pacific steam. Developments decades hence, however, would see a CPR steam locomotive return to service under company ownership when H1b Hudson No. 2816 was repatriated to Canada from long-time display at Steamtown. ROBERT F. COLLINS, MORNING SUN BOOKS COLLECTION

BELOW: A more antiquated consist was in evidence at Ste. Thérèse on October 4, 1959, trailing D4g No. 424. ROBERT F. COLLINS, MORNING SUN BOOKS COLLECTION

LEFT: Class G1s Pacific No. 2222, leading an NRHS excursion, paused at Lachute on September 2, 1951. The 4-6-2 was an MLW product delivered to the CPR in February 1911 as G1d No. 1022, and retired in late 1956. During the stop, fans scrambled to record the arrival of Ottawa–Montreal Train No. 422 behind Pacific No. 1262, a G5c built by CLC in November 1946 and firmly at the opposite end of the CPR's 4-6-2 spectrum. BOTH, SANDY GOODRICK

ABOVE: Train No. 131 was a morning run on the CPR's 125.6-mile Montreal–Ottawa route running north of the Ottawa River via the Lachute Subdivision. "Dayliners" had become regulars in this service by the time RDC-1 No. 9066 and RDC-2 No. 9106 called at Staynerville, Quebec, on October 4, 1959.

LEFT: At Lachute on the same day, Ottawa–Montreal "Dayliner" Train No. 132, with RDC-2 No. 9111 leading, passed alongside the excursion consist led by D4g No. 424. Having departed Ottawa's Union Station at 7:45 that morning, the Budd cars would deliver their Montreal-bound passengers to Windsor Station, not quite 50 miles ahead, at 10:50am. BOTH, ROBERT F. COLLINS, MORNING SUN BOOKS COLLECTION

ABOVE: Soon after Train No. 131's RDC's departed on October 4, 1959, CPR D4g No. 424 passed Staynerville with the CRHA excursion. ROBERT F. COLLINS, MORNING SUN BOOKS COLLECTION

BELOW AND BOTTOM: Locomotive and consist that day provided a glimpse of the CPR's not-so-distant past. BOTH, AUTHOR'S COLLECTION

ABOVE: Motorcading vehicles—themselves destined to become objects of nostalgic affection—choked the roads paralleling No. 424's October 4, 1959, excursion over the Lachute Sub. AUTHOR'S COLLECTION

LEFT: The westbound NRHS excursion led by G1s Pacific No. 2222—and complete with Midwest Chapter drumhead sign—was stopped at Calumet, Quebec, on September 2, 1951. SANDY GOODRICK

BOTTOM AND OVERLEAF: Given the disdain which many crews held for the CPR's D4g class, pity the hard-working fireman on the CRHA's October 4, 1959, excursion. He put on a good show, though, for railfans and photographers west of Calumet at the Lachute Subdivision's Rivière Rouge crossing. ROBERT F. COLLINS, MORNING SUN BOOKS COLLECTION

OPPOSITE TOP: The phrase "going out in a blaze of glory" would certainly seem an apt description of D4g No. 424's excursion activity on October 3-4, 1959, and in particular of the engine's amble along the CPR's Lachute Subdivision on the 4th. Railfans crane for a better view from the open combine door at Pointe au Chene, Quebec.

LEFT: The rustic log-and-stone CPR station at Montebello hinted at the recreational pursuits to be found in the nearby Laurentien mountains.

ABOVE: A more direct appeal for tourist's dollars was evident as No. 424 led its train near Plaisance on October 4, 1959.

ALL, ROBERT F. COLLINS, MORNING SUN BOOKS COLLECTION

TOP: During the course of their September 2, 1951, Montreal–Ottawa outing behind G1s Pacific No. 2222, members of the Midwest Chapter NRHS stretched their legs on the platform at Buckingham Junction, Quebec, the point at which the 3.2-mile Buckingham Subdivision joined the Lachute Sub.

MIDDLE: Upholstered walkover seating gave a hint of modernity to the NRHS train's elderly but well-maintained rolling stock.

BOTTOM: Equally well-maintained trackage receded from the rear car west of Calumet.

ALL, SANDY GOODRICK;

TICKET ENVELOPE, AUTHOR'S COLLECTION

Enjoyed by fans and encouraged by a receptive management, excursions were plentiful on Canadian Pacific, particularly in Quebec and southern Ontario, as steam passed from the landscape. One of the many locomotives to hold fantrip assignments in the waning years was G2u Pacific No. 2663, built in the railway's Angus Shops in April 1914 as a member of class G2f, and reclassified at a 1924 shopping. It was scrapped in February 1961.
BOTH, AUTHOR'S COLLECTION

More fantrip variety as the curtain fell on Canadian Pacific steam. The locomotives pictured here include G5c Pacific No. 1271 (CLC, April 1947) leading H1c Royal Hudson No. 2839 (MLW, Sept. 1937) in September 1958; P1d Mikado No. 5118 (Angus, Oct. 1912) and P1n 2-8-2 No. 5214 (built by MLW in 1912 as a 2-8-0 and one of 65 converted to P1n Mikados by the CPR after World War II) in September 1959; and D10h No. 1098 (CLC, Nov. 1913) in September 1959. Of these examples, two escaped scrapping. Royal Hudson No. 2839 initially was preserved in Ontario, and later enjoyed a brief resurrection in excursion service in the U.S. Southeast in the late 1970s; No. 1098 was also a survivor, preserved at Steamtown. ALL, AUTHOR'S COLLECTION

OPPOSITE TOP: One last look at CPR D4g No. 424, this time taking water at St. Jean on October 3, 1959. ROBERT F. COLLINS, MORNING SUN BOOKS COLLECTION

OPPOSITE BOTTOM: During its April 14, 1960, mileage on behalf of the CRHA, G5a No. 1201 crossed the wide Richelieu River at St. Jean. ROBERT F. COLLINS, MORNING SUN BOOKS COLLECTION

TOP RIGHT: Junctions abounded south of Montreal, as various CPR and CNR routes headed east and south, and several U.S. lines reached north to what was for decades Canada's largest city. St. Jean was a busy crossroads; CPR G2u No. 2658 worked a local freight there on November 24, 1956. GEORGE DIMOND

MIDDLE RIGHT AND BELOW: At aptly named Delson, Delaware & Hudson subsidiary Napierville Junction connected with the CPR; Canadian Pacific G2s No. 2541 led a wayfreight through town on May 9, 1959. BOTH, ROBERT F. COLLINS, MORNING SUN BOOKS COLLECTION

MONTREAL
Heart and Soul

Symbolizing both progress and resistance to changes sweeping through the industry at large, the semi-streamlined steam locomotives built for the CPR under the mechanical direction of motive power chief Henry Bowen are icons of Canadian railroading. Best known, by virtue of their relatively large number and regal pedigree, were the 45 Royal Hudsons; they were "titled" by virtue of the exemplary record of one of their number, H1d No. 2850, during the Royal Tour of King George VI and Queen Elizabeth in 1939. Cast crowns on their forward running boards were a permanent reminder of the honor. Running out its last miles, H1c No. 2822 had been reduced to hauling Montreal commuter trains when it led inbound Train No. 274 from Vaudreuil on March 23, 1960.
ROBERT F. COLLINS, MORNING SUN BOOKS COLLECTION

Canadian Pacific's headquarters city for more than a century, Montreal's location on the St. Lawrence River guaranteed its development as a strategic transportation cossroads. Until the 1959 opening of the St. Lawrence Seaway, the Lachine Rapids, adjacent to Montreal, was the easternmost impediment blocking ocean-going ships from access to the Great Lakes, and similarly prevented all but the smallest "lakers" from continuing downstream via the antiquated Lachine Canal.

With grain, timber, and other exports figuring largely in Montreal's late 19th century economy, merchants and politicians early on backed rail links to Atlantic ports that, unlike Montreal's, were ice-free year-round. The CPR's winter outlet for Montreal's commerce was Saint John, N.B., while CNR predecessor Grand Trunk developed its own ice-free port facilities at Portland, Maine.

For both the CPR and CNR, and exemplified particularly in the two roads' long-distance passenger schedules, Montreal became a divider between eastern and western operations. Transcontinental passenger trains from Vancouver traveled almost 3,000 miles east to Montreal, but no further. Passengers bound to and from the Maritime Provinces were obliged to transfer to trains running between the Atlantic coast and Montreal, but no further west.

With the city's core located on an island in the wide and fast-flowing St. Lawrence, Montreal's railroads depended on substantial bridges for access to main lines reaching in all directions.

Canadian Pacific trains serving Quebec's Eastern Townships, the Maritime Provinces, and New England—along with trackage-rights tenants Delaware & Hudson and New York Central—crossed the St. Lawrence a few miles upstream from Montreal on this massive double-track span. Class G5c Pacific No. 1258, built by CLC in November 1946, leads Train No. 213 north across the structure early on the morning of May 9, 1959. This daily-except-Sunday local schedule originated at Farnham, 43.2 miles from Windsor Station, and, in concert with its afternoon opposite number 214 (No. 218 on Fridays) provided a commuter-friendly timing to and from Montreal.
ROBERT F. COLLINS, MORNING SUN BOOKS COLLECTION

OPPOSITE: Farnham–Montreal Train No. 213's consist on May 9, 1959, included a trio of express cars ahead of the requisite local coaches. At this point in its one hour and 25 minute run it was a few hundred feet short of the St. Lawrence's north shore. Ahead lay stops at LaSalle, Montreal West, and Westmount, before a 7:00am arrival at Windsor Station. Upon leaving Adirondack Junction on the river's south shore, the train fell under the operational jurisdiction of the CPR's Montreal Terminals.

THIS PAGE: Viewed from the opposite end of the St. Lawrence River bridge, G5a No. 1201 approaches the CPR's Adirondack Junction with a CRHA excursion train on March 23, 1960. Landfall from the main bridge will be followed by a crossing, via recently installed vertical lift spans, of the newly opened St. Lawrence Seaway. The joint U.S.-Canadian waterway indirectly precipitated the end of CPR and CNR steam in the East, since the greater inland range afforded to ocean freighters ("Salties") caused a rail traffic downturn and motive power surplus. Diesels then on-hand were ample for the rail traffic available, effectively sealing the fate of the steam locomotives and service facilities still in operation. ALL, ROBERT F. COLLINS, MORNING SUN BOOKS COLLECTION

Windsor Station served both as headquarters and primary Montreal passenger terminal for the Canadian Pacific well beyond the end of the steam era. The turreted-and-towered Richardsonian Romanesque landmark was erected in stages, the first of which opened in 1889. Windsor Station's original designs were executed by architect Bruce Price, who went on to design the railway's first Banff Springs Hotel and Quebec City's Chateau Frontenac. The portion of Windsor Station visible here, an office and tower block built facing Windsor Street, was designed by architects J.W.H. Watts, L.F. Taylor, and W.S. Painter and built between 1910 and 1915. Additions to the station were being made as late as 1954. On August 19, 1958, G3h Pacific No. 2426 led Train No. 181 out from the train shed and into its 25.6-mile afternoon run to Ste. Thérèse. ROBERT F. COLLINS, MORNING SUN BOOKS COLLECTION

OPPOSITE: Servicing of passenger trains originating and terminating at Windsor Station was performed at Glen Yard (commonly known as "the Glen"), two miles west of the terminal opposite the CPR's Westmount station. Inbound trains had to back out of stub-ended Windsor Station and up the short grade to Westmount, like this one behind H1c Royal Hudson No. 2821 did on March 29, 1958. BOTH, ROBERT F. COLLINS, MORNING SUN BOOKS COLLECTION

ABOVE: On the same day, G5c Pacific No. 1258 arrived at Windsor Station with four-car Train No. 213 from Farnham. ROBERT F. COLLINS, MORNING SUN BOOKS COLLECTION

BELOW: Class N2a Consolidation No. 3642 was assigned to Windsor Station switching duties in October 1958. The 2-8-0 was built by MLW in 1911 as N3a No. 1842, becoming No. 3842 in 1912 until finally reclassified and renumbered in 1927. AUTHOR'S COLLECTION

OPPOSITE TOP: G5b Pacific No. 1229 lifted a short local train away from Windsor Station on March 29, 1958.

LEFT: Adorned with Bowen's distinctive front-end styling, G3j Pacific No. 2470 (MLW, July 1948) was among the last Pacifics built for the CPR. On March 29, 1958, it backed out to the Glen for turning. BOTH, ROBERT F. COLLINS, MORNING SUN BOOKS COLLECTION

ABOVE: H1c Royal Hudson No. 2821 was built by MLW in 1937. AUTHOR'S COLLECTION

BELOW: With its flue time about to expire, in late 1959 A2q 4-4-0 No. 144 was returned from New Brunswick to Montreal, where it led a couple of excursions that November before retirement and donation to the CRHA. ROBERT F. COLLINS, MORNING SUN BOOKS COLLECTION

ABOVE: N2A Consolidation No. 3642 was a Windsor Station regular in the late 1950s, conveying cuts of passenger and express cars between the Glen and the CPR's downtown terminal, as in this view from May 29, 1957. GEORGE DIMOND

BELOW: Standing out among the maroon cars in this March 1958 transfer is one of the 22 heavyweight 14-section sleeping cars modernized and sheathed in Budd stainless steel fluting for assignment to *The Canadian*, the CPR's domeliner flagship. These *U*-series sleepers were used in tourist service between 1955 and 1965. ROBERT F. COLLINS, MORNING SUN BOOKS COLLECTION

OPPOSITE TOP: H1c Royal Hudson No. 2821 and G3h Pacific No. 2426 back toward Windsor Station on August 19, 1958, while, in the distance, an Alco-design diesel switcher lugs a string of passenger cars through the terminal's throat trackage.

OPPOSITE BOTTOM: Bowen's Royal Hudson styling kept the engines' jackets and skylines remarkably free of appurtenances and other clutter. A low-profile, saddle-style sandbox was hidden beneath the planished cylindrical jacket, which also concealed the same tapered boiler used on the CPR's earlier non-streamlined Hudsons. BOTH, ROBERT F. COLLINS, MORNING SUN BOOKS COLLECTION

RIGHT: When the CPR opened Canada's first modern hump yard at Montreal in July 1950, provision still had to be made for steam power. St. Luc Yard's ponderous concrete coaling station loomed over P1e 2-8-2 No. 5163 on March 23, 1958.

BELOW: Sister P1e Mikado No. 5162, built by MLW in August 1913 as P1b No. 5062, awaited its next assignment at St. Luc on March 29, 1958.

BOTTOM: No. 5114 was a member of the CPR's P1d class. Shown at Montreal on March 29, 1958, the 2-8-2 had been built at Angus Shops in September 1912 as P1a No. 5014.

ALL, ROBERT F. COLLINS, MORNING SUN BOOKS COLLECTION

ABOVE: Gleaming G3g Pacific No. 2408 was ready to head to Windsor Station from the Glen for its next outbound run on June 24, 1958. The 4-6-2 was delivered by CLC in November 1942, and met its end in March 1961. ROBERT F. COLLINS, MORNING SUN BOOKS COLLECTION

MIDDLE: Although Delaware & Hudson's semi-streamlined Northerns had once been regular visitors to the CPR's Glen Yard, laying over between assignments on the Montreal–New York City schedules operated by D&H in conjunction with New York Central, dieselization of the D&H's cross-border passenger operations meant that black-and-yellow, boiler-equipped Alco RS units became daily visitors to the Glen. On September 6, 1953, H1c Royal Hudson No. 2823 shared a track with one of the D&H's newcomers. GEORGE DIMOND

BOTTOM: A pair of D&H Alcos negotiates trackage at the Glen in December 1959, prior to returning home via the Napierville Junction connection at Delson. AUTHOR'S COLLECTION

123

ABOVE: CPR Train No. 180, a weekday-only local run from Ste. Thérèse, headed through Montreal West on its way in to Windsor Station on March 23, 1960, behind G3h Pacific No. 2426 (CLC, Sept. 1944).

RIGHT AND OPPOSITE TOP: As was the case with Canadian National's streamlined U-4-a Northerns, several of Canadian Pacific's widely admired Royal Hudsons ended their careers hauling commuter trains. The CPR maintained a well-patronized suburban service linking Montreal's "West Island" communites with the city, and in was in that capacity that H1c No. 2825 led Train No. 246 from Vaudreuil toward Windsor Station on March 23, 1960. ALL, ROBERT F. COLLINS, MORNING SUN BOOKS COLLECTION

About as far from its former glories as it could be while remaining under steam, H1b Hudson No. 2811 worked a 33-car freight transfer through Montreal on March 23, 1960. Even at this late date, almost three full decades after it had left its MLW birthplace in November 1930, the Hudson's understated passenger livery endured. Although scrapping came for No. 2811 in July 1961, sister No. 2816 survived as the only preserved example of Bowen's original CPR Hudsons; in 2005, it is again under steam and owned by Canadian Pacific. ROBERT F. COLLINS, MORNING SUN BOOKS COLLECTION; TIMETABLE AND MAP, AUTHOR'S COLLECTION

CANADIAN PACIFIC RAILWAY

ATLANTIC REGION
MONTREAL TERMINALS DIVISION

 TIME **31** TABLE

TAKING EFFECT at 12.01 a.m., SUNDAY, OCTOBER 25th, 1959

GOVERNED BY EASTERN STANDARD TIME

FOR THE INFORMATION AND GUIDANCE OF EMPLOYEES ONLY

J. R. STROTHER, GENERAL MANAGER

F. A. POULIOT, ASSISTANT GENERAL MANAGER

J. B. MACPHERSON, SUPERINTENDENT TRANSPORTATION

RIGHT: Like a steaming cyclops, H1c Royal Hudson No. 2826 squints into the sun in October 1958. AUTHOR'S COLLECTION

BELOW: Heading into a literal *and* figurative sunset of its own, G3h Pacific No. 2426—a war baby built by CLC in 1944—led Train No. 181 west out of Montreal's Windsor Station on August 19, 1958. ROBERT F. COLLINS, MORNING SUN BOOKS COLLECTION

CANADIAN PACIFIC STEAM IN COLOR, VOL. 2 *by Kevin J. Holland*
Enjoy more great vintage CPR steam images, from Montreal west to the Rocky Mountains.